A **BEACON** ❊ BIOGRAPHY

# CHADWICK BOSEMAN

### Pete DiPrimio

PURPLE TOAD
PUBLISHING

Printing     1          2          3          4          5          6          7          8          9

## A Beacon Biography

Angelina Jolie
Anthony Davis
Big Time Rush
Bill Nye
Cam Newton
Carly Rae Jepsen
Carson Wentz
Chadwick Boseman
Daisy Ridley
Drake
Ed Sheeran
Ellen DeGeneres
Elon Musk
Ezekiel Elliott
Gal Gadot
Harry Styles of One Direction
Jennifer Lawrence

John Boyega
Kevin Durant
Lorde
Malala
Maria von Trapp
Markus "Notch" Persson, Creator of Minecraft
Millie Bobby Brown
Misty Copeland
Mo'ne Davis
Muhammad Ali
Neil deGrasse Tyson
Peyton Manning
Robert Griffin III (RG3)
Stephen Colbert
Stephen Curry
Tom Holland
Zendaya

**Publisher's Cataloging-in-Publication Data**
DiPrimio, Pete.
   Chadwick Boseman / written by Pete DiPrimio.
     p. cm.
Includes bibliographic references, glossary, and index.
ISBN 9781624693878
1. Actors—United States—Biography—Juvenile literature. 2. Superheroes—Juvenile literature. I. Series: Beacon biography.
 PN2287 2017
 791.4092
                  **Library of Congress Control Number:** 201795779

**eBook ISBN:** 9781624693885

**ABOUT THE AUTHOR:** Pete DiPrimio is an award-winning sportswriter, a long-time author and freelance writer, and a member of the Indiana Sportswriters and Sports Broadcasters Hall of Fame. He's been an adjunct lecturer for the National Sports Journalism Center at IUPU-Indianapolis and for Indiana University's School of Journalism. He is the author of three nonfiction books pertaining to Indiana University athletics, a coauthor of another book on IU athletics, and author of more than two dozen children's books. His book on the IU 2017 football season and coach Tom Allen is set for publication in 2018. He is seeking an agent for his first novel, a sports thriller. Pete is also a fitness instructor, plus a tennis, racquetball, biking, and weight-lifting enthusiast.

**PUBLISHER'S NOTE:** This story has not been authorized or endorsed by Chadwick Boseman.

# CONTENTS

Chadwick Boseman drew a big crowd of fans who wanted him to sign their Black Panther movie posters.

Chadwick Boseman is no superhero.

Except that he is.

Why?

Because he's Black Panther.

Actually, Chadwick is the actor who plays Black Panther, one of the most popular of the Marvel Comics superheroes, and the first black superhero to star in his own Marvel movie: *Black Panther*.

This means Chadwick, who is called Chad by his friends, has all sorts of special movie powers. At least, Black Panther does.

Invented by Marvel creators Stan Lee and Jack Kirby in 1966, Black Panther is super fast, strong, and agile. He doesn't get tired. He has awesome vision, hearing, and smell. His powers come from eating a special herb, called the heart-shaped herb, which is found in Black Panther's fictional African country of Wakanda, a place that is magically hidden from the rest of the world.

*Jack Kirby (right) cocreated Thor, Hulk, Iron Man, Captain America and the X-Men with Stan Lee.*

Black Panther, whose real name is T'Challa in the Marvel Universe, is also one of the smartest people on Earth. He's a scientist, an inventor, and the leader of his country. He wears a very cool, special suit with retractable claws (like a panther). It is made of vibranium, an out-of-this-world metal.

It really is out of this world. According to Marvel legend, vibranium comes from a meteorite that smashed into Earth 10,000 years ago. A big chunk of it landed in Wakanda. Because vibranium absorbs sound waves and other vibrations, it is stronger than normal metal. The shield of another Marvel superhero, Captain America, is also made of it.

Vibranium could be used to make dangerous weapons for bad guys, which is why Black Panther keeps his country hidden. He doesn't want the metal used to hurt people.

Growing up, Boseman knew some things about this character and his world, but he had to learn a lot more when he won the acting role. He would play Black Panther in at least five movies. His debut of the character came in the 2016 hit *Captain America: Civil War*. He also appears in *Avengers: Infinity War*.

Not only does Boseman play a superhero, he also has to speak like someone who comes

**Fans got into the Black Panther look, even wearing the costume.**

from Wakanda. He had to learn to talk with an accent that doesn't really exist.

How did he do that?

Boseman worked with a language coach to help him with the accent. It is based on the way a group of people from South Africa, called the Xhosa (HO-suh), talk. They also listened to how people talk in Kenya, Ethiopia, and Sierra Leone. They mixed these together and made up a new accent.

Boseman would sometimes try out the accent while he was in disguise to keep from being recognized, he told the *Los Angeles Times*. "That's how you stay fresh with it."[1]

*Director Ryan Coogler, who had a hit with his Rocky boxing movie, Creed, expected big things by directing Black Panther.*

Black Panther battles many villians in the movie. These fight scenes are intense and take a lot of energy. To get fired up, Boseman and *Black Panther* director Ryan Coogler sometimes mixed it up before the filming started. Boseman told *Vulture.com* that Coogler would spar with him, "throwin' punches and kicks at each other."[2]

Playing Black Panther gave a big boost to Boseman's movie career, just as Captain America did for Chris Evans, Spiderman did for Tom Holland, Thor did for Chris Hemsworth, and Star-Lord Peter Quill did for Chris Pratt.

Boseman's career has gone far beyond a movie superhero. Some consider him the African American version of versatile actor Leonardo DiCaprio. Others call him the "Ebony Chameleon" (EH-buh-nee kuh-MEEL-yun) because he can play so many kinds of roles and change his appearance so often.

A lot of actors wanted to be Black Panther. How did Boseman get the part? What made him the right person for that role, and so many others?

# Chapter 2

## Early Years

*In 1993, Boseman played guard on his T. J. Hanna High School basketball team in Anderson, South Carolina. The historic Anderson County Courthouse was built in 1898 and is a landmark building in the area.*

Chadwick Boseman was born on November 29, 1976, in Anderson, South Carolina. His father, Leroy, owned an upholstery business. Workers there put stuffing, springs, and covers on chairs and couches. His mother, Carolyn, was a nurse. An African ancestry DNA test showed that Chadwick's ancestors came from the African country of Sierra Leone.[1]

Chadwick played some Little League Baseball growing up, but he was mostly a year-round basketball player. At T. L. Hanna High School in Anderson, he was on the basketball and cross-country teams. He was also a key member of the school's speech and debate team, as well as the National Forensic League, a national debate and speech organization for students. Beyond that, he was an honor student and a member of the National Honor Society. He graduated in 1995.

Chadwick grew up wanting to be a movie director and writer. He graduated from Howard University in Washington, D.C., with a bachelor of fine arts in directing. One of his drama teachers at Howard was the actress Phylicia Rashad. Chadwick also attended the British American Drama Academy in London, England. In order to better understand actors, he took acting lessons. He also studied digital filmmaking—how to use digital cameras and computers to edit videos—at New York City's Digital Film Academy.

While in New York, Boseman was the drama instructor at the Schomburg Junior Scholars Program in Harlem from 2002 to 2007. He also did some acting. His first television role came in 2003 for an episode of *Third Watch*. He also appeared in series such as *Law & Order*, *ER*, and *CSI: NY*.

Meanwhile, he wrote a play called *Deep Azure*. It appeared at Chicago's Congo Square Theatre Company. The play is based on the true story of a Howard University student killed by police. In 2006, *Deep Azure* was nominated for the Joseph Jefferson Award, which honors excellence in Chicago-area theater.

For ten years Chadwick mixed stage directing and writing plays with acting roles. He was still more interested in writing and directing, but he kept showing a lot of promise as an actor. He hired an agency to help him

**Boseman didn't shy away from hard-hitting topics in his writing. His play Deep Azure *touched on racism and police brutality.***

get roles, and one of the agents told him that he had to choose between being an actor and being a director/playwright. He had been doing both for years—and was struggling to make money. He lived in a small New York apartment and took poor-paying jobs at theater companies. It was tough to pay his rent and other bills.

"I think the most stressful time of my life was when I was in New York and I didn't have money to pay my rent," he told *GQ* magazine. "I was going to the mailbox every day waiting for the check to come.

"When you don't have money, when you've got, like, a jar full of change and each day it's 'Okay, I've got enough to get on the train' and 'Maybe that check's gonna come today . . .'. There's nothing more stressful than your stomach growling."[3]

Stressed or not, Chadwick said he did some of his best writing while being "poor and hungry."[4]

By 2008, he knew he needed a change. He wanted to act—and to make enough money to eat well and pay the bills—so he moved to Los Angeles. There, he appeared in multiple episodes of the TV show *Lincoln Heights*. Also that year, he appeared in his first movie, the sports drama *The Express*. Two years later, he was a regular for the TV show *Persons Unknown*.

Despite these roles, Boseman felt he wasn't really making it. He had auditioned for some major movie roles and hadn't gotten them. He was hoping to get the role of former Major League Baseball legend Jackie Robinson for the movie *42*, but months went by without any callbacks. He thought about giving up acting and returning to New York to write and direct again.

Before he made up his mind, he went to a New York City bar to watch the St. Louis Cardinals win a playoff game. Suddenly a feeling hit—he was going to get the Jackie Robinson role.

"The next night [movie producers] called me," Chadwick told *GQ*. "Just like—boom!—it's yours."[5]

Boseman had never had a starring role in a movie before. That was about to change.

Boseman goes all out when preparing to play a character—or in talking about it.

In 2011, Boseman faced heat hotter than any fastball. Rachel Robinson was the wife of Baseball Hall of Famer Jackie Robinson, the man who broke the color barrier in professional baseball. She made it clear that Boseman was not her choice to play her husband in a movie about his world-changing life. She wanted Sidney Poitier or Denzel Washington, famous Academy Award–winning actors, to do it. But by the time the movie was to be made, those actors were too old.

So at age 37, and with a background that included baseball, basketball, and boxing, Boseman got the opportunity of a lifetime. He had the appearance and physical skills needed to play one of the best baseball players of all time. He also had the acting talent to pull it off.

Still, Rachel wasn't sure.

"I didn't know if a young actor who was getting into a major production for the first time could convey him," she told Sean Gregory of *Time*.[1]

Rachel was blunter with Boseman. He told *Flaunt.com*, "She said 'Well, if we had made this movie when we were supposed to make this movie, Sidney Poitier would have played Jackie and then Denzel was supposed to play him. Now, we have you. So who are you?'

"You have to brace yourself for that right there."[2]

**Jackie and Rachel Robinson met when they were both at UCLA in the early 1940s. They were married in 1946 and had three children—two boys and a girl.**

Meanwhile fall was inching toward winter in 2011, and this much Chadwick knew: It had been a tough year. He kept striking out on acting parts that could have really launched his career, including the Oscar-nominated movie *Django Unchained* directed by Quentin Tarantino. As Boseman told *Entertainment Weekly*, "I had tested for so many, like, over five major roles—roles that you would be like, 'Oh, that could change your life.' And I didn't get it. So I had become frustrated with that."[3]

Boseman had only been in one movie and that was a small role in 2008's *The Express*. TV roles in ABC Family's *Lincoln Heights* and NBC's *Persons Unknown* hadn't made him a household name. He had never played a leading man anywhere, let alone in a major movie, and playing Jackie Robinson would be the ultimate leading-man experience.

Tarantino didn't pick Boseman for his movie, but he was very impressed. According to *Time*, after Boseman's audition, Tarantino said, "That guy is going to be something."[4]

Boseman had a great audition for *42* director Brian Helgeland. He did a scene in which he played Jackie Robinson having to take it when Philadelphia Phillies manager Ben Chapman insulted him repeatedly with racial slurs. Robinson didn't flinch on the field, but afterward he smashed a bat and broke down in tears.

"It was such a brave choice [for the audition]," Helgeland told *Time*. "I thought right away, 'This is the guy.' "[5]

*Philadelphia manager Ben Chapman (right) publicly insulted and demeaned Robinson because he didn't believe African Americans should play Major League Baseball. A photo was taken afterward to make the public think everything was forgiven. It was not.*

*Besides baseball, Jackie Robinson was a track star at UCLA. He won the 1940 NCAA title in the long jump. He also played football and basketball for the Bruins.*

Boseman also had to do a baseball tryout at UCLA's Jackie Robinson Stadium. (Robinson had attended UCLA in the 1940s.) Boseman thrived at the workout and everything else. He learned all of Robinson's habits, including the way he put his hands on his hips as if he ran the show.

The fact that he wasn't a well-known star helped because, as Helgeland told *Time*, he didn't want a big name. "I have a much easier time buying into the whole thing when the actor is not very well known. [Otherwise] the audience is trying to get past the person they know and into the movie."[6]

Boseman knew *42* could be his breakthrough. And it was.

Boseman was able to work with Harrison Ford, famous for *Star Wars* (as Han Solo) and *Indiana Jones*. Ford played Branch Rickey, the president and general manager of the Brooklyn Dodgers. Rickey forever ended segregation in Major League Baseball when he signed Robinson in 1947. During filming, Boseman also met former major league home-run king Hank Aaron.

Boseman spent five months training for baseball the way it was played in the late 1940s. He practiced twice a day and worked with college and professional coaches. Movie officials would film him batting and compare it with old film of Robinson hitting so that Boseman could do it exactly the way Robinson did it. They did the same thing with his fielding and base running.

"I could see how bad I was and how good he was," Boseman jokingly told Julie Miller of *Vanity Fair*.[7]

**The movie 42 was shown at the White House for President Barack Obama. Boseman was there along with fellow actor Harrison Ford and Rachel Robinson.**

A lot of people would tell Boseman what a hero Jackie Robinson was, but Boseman wanted to show him as a man. "I thought, Let me just focus on the truth," he told Miller.[8]

In the end, the truth made all the difference.

Rachel Robinson was 90 years old when she saw the movie. She gave Boseman a big thumb's up.

"I was thrilled by Chad's depiction of Jack," she told *Time*. "I was moved to tears by the performance. I felt the warmth and passion that Jack and I felt for each other. It's quietly portrayed. I cherished it so much."[9]

*Flaunt.com* asked Boseman whether Rachel Robinson still wondered if he was the right actor for the job. Boseman replied, "I think we're good now."[10]

*Like many actors, Boseman attended the Academy Award ceremony dressed to impress.*

Boseman thought about turning down his next role. He could have said no. He'd done one movie about a historical African American figure—Jackie Robinson. He didn't want to do another. He said he didn't want to be stuck in those kind of roles forever and not get a chance to do anything else.[1]

But somehow, he kept doing them.

Boseman wound up taking the role of legendary African American rock singer James Brown. He also auditioned for a movie about another legendary African American rock star, the late Jimi Hendrix. And then he took the role of Thurgood Marshall, the first African American Supreme Court Justice, and one of the key figures in the civil rights movement.

"Some people have said, 'You don't need to do any more biopics,' but I don't agree with that," Boseman told the *Michigan Chronicle*. "A lot of our [African American] stories haven't been told."[2]

James Brown, known as the Godfather of Soul, was a force of nature in music. From the early 1950s into the twenty-first century, he powered his way through songs with enough energy for ten men. Boseman tapped into that energy while playing Brown in *Get On Up*. Although he sang in the movie, including concert scenes, the public never heard it. Brown's actual voice was dubbed in for the movie.

**Legendary performer James Brown was known as the hardest working man in show business during his long career. Boseman played Brown in the movie, Get On Up.**

Still, Boseman told the *Santa Barbara Independent,* "I got to feel like a rock star."[3]

Once he landed the role, Boseman prepared by listening to all of Brown's records and watching as much film of him as he could. He listened to so much of it, he joked, that after a while he avoided all of Brown's songs and anything that sounded like him. He also interviewed Brown's family, read books about him, and took five-hour dance classes.

Boseman also decided to practice what a James Brown concert would look like for the movie. That included wearing wigs and costumes. Choreographer

Aakomon Jones came up with dance moves. Boseman sang and danced as if it were an actual concert.

"It was an intense amount of work just to see, 'What would this look like if we did it?'" Boseman told *Entertainment Weekly.* "I had no idea how it would turn out."[4]

It turned out very well.

Then there was his turn as Thurgood Marshall, an attorney who helped end segregation. During this period of U.S.

**Boseman appeared in France for a screening of the movie Get On Up with Rolling Stones superstar Mick Jagger (left) and movie producer Brian Grazer. Jagger and Grazer were two of the film's producers.**

history, African Americans and whites were not allowed to share public places. For example, African American students couldn't go to white schools. In 1967, Marshall became the first African-American Supreme Court Justice.

In the movie *Marshall*, Boseman plays a young Marshall who takes the case of a black servant accused of attacking a wealthy white woman. It was a fight against bigotry that Marshall had battled his whole life. As Marshall once said, "The only way to get through a bigot's door is to break it down."[5]

Adding to the challenge of defending the black servant,

*Thurgood Marshall played a huge role in the civil rights movement as a lawyer. He then served as the first African American Supreme Court justice.*

Marshall was not allowed to talk during the trial because of his race. An inexperienced Jewish attorney was hired to do the talking in court.

"The thing I loved the most was the fact that [Marshall] had to work the case without talking," Boseman told the *Michigan Chronicle*. "He's gagged. It's like being a boxer with one hand tied behind your back."[6]

Gagged or not, Marshall—and Boseman—did what needed to be done. The same was true for James Brown and Boseman's performance of him. And for those wishing Boseman had won an acting award for his *Get On Up* performance, he had this thought: "When it comes down to it," he told the *Santa Barbara Independent*, "I'd rather have an action figure than a Golden Globe."[7]

*Boseman got to flex his superhero muscles with fellow* Avengers: Infinity War *costars Chris Hemsworth, who plays Thor, and Josh Brolin, who plays Thanos.*

## No Time to Rest

Once fame found him, Boseman began helping out.

In 2017, Hurricane Harvey devastated Houston, Texas. Boseman used social media to encourage his fans to donate.

He tweeted, *"So many ways we can all help... @shelterboxusa | @RedCross | @JJWatt www.youcaring.com/jjwat... #HurricaneHarvey pic.twitter.com/G5MbjJD."*[1]

He followed with another tweet: *"My prayers go out to the 30,000 who need aid in #Texas. Please help @shelterboxusa provide relief: http://shelterboxusa.org #harvey."*[2]

He also posted a Facebook video asking fans to help.

Fame could have put Chadwick in the spotlight . . . but did it?

His acting versatility let him play a number of different roles without drawing true movie star attention. As he told the *Santa Barbara Independent*, "The funny thing is these are all such different roles; I am able to walk down the streets without being noticed."[3]

Noticed or not, Boseman tried to take the advice of legendary African American singer/actor Harry Belafonte. He stressed that movies have the power to change society if you're willing to use them. Boseman's roles,

**Harry Belafonte (left) had a big impact on Boseman just as famous civil rights leader Martin Luther King Jr. (right) had on Belafonte during the 1960s.**

including that of Black Panther, have given him the chance to generate change.

"I feel like to a certain degree, [Belafonte] gives you marching orders," Boseman told *Entertainment Weekly*. "So I got some marching orders."[4]

Fame helped Chadwick learn who his real friends are. He told *GQ* that he cut back on the number of his friends. "I've closed things down. No new friends. [Hanging out with friends] could be distracting. My circle is a lot less open now."[5]

When you get rich and famous, Boseman said, "some people, who under normal circumstances might be out of your life, they all come back."[6]

Through it all, Boseman has kept thinking about writing and directing. Actor Chris Evans, who plays Captain America, used his fame to direct a movie. Boseman said he could see himself doing the same thing. He said he's interested in being a "complete artist."[7] Acting is only a part of that.

There is nothing fake in Boseman, whether it's singing, dancing, acting, or writing. For him, it's all about the truth of the performance.

Boseman approaches each role the way an athlete does a workout or a competition. That was especially true of *Get On Up* and *42*. He told *GQ*, "These roles kill my body. When we were doing *42*, I don't think people

**Boseman prepared to make an awards presentation with fellow Avengers: Infinity Wars star Chris Evans.**

really get how extensive the training was. The conditioning sessions were madness with how hard it was."

"[On *42*], they would shoot each moment [many times to get different camera angles]. So if I stole a base, I had to steal it four or five times just to have what they needed. And something might have gone wrong with the camera; something might have gone wrong with the person who's supposed to catch the ball; something might have gone wrong with me. So I did some takes, I know, fifty times. Then again, I did the splits ninety-six times one day on *Get On Up*. That particular day was probably harder than any baseball day, but the average baseball day, wow."[8]

Success might make some people want to take it easy. Not Boseman. He has too many things he wants to do.

*With plenty of Black Panther movies coming, Boseman will be busy signing Black Panther items years to come.*

"I don't think I've done my best work yet," he told *GQ*. "It ain't no time to rest."[9]

Or, as he tweeted this quote from former Czech Republic president and writer Vaclav Havel: "The real test of a man is not when he plays the role that he wants for himself, but when he plays the role destiny has for him."[10]

His fans are right there with him, wondering what role destiny will bring him next.

**1976**   Chadwick Boseman is born on November 29 in Anderson, South Carolina.

**1995**   He graduates from T. L. Hanna High School as a member of the National Honor Society.

**1996**   He enters Howard University in Washington, D.C., and earns a bachelor's degree in fine arts and directing in 2000.

**2000**   He studies at the British American Drama Academy in London, England.

**2001**   Boseman takes digital filmmaking classes at New York City's Digital Film Academy.

**2002**   He begins teaching drama at the Schomburg Junior Scholars Program in Harlem.

**2003**   He begins getting small parts on TV series such as *Third Watch*, *Law & Order*, *ER*, and *CSI: NY*.

**2006**   His play *Deep Azure* is nominated for the Joseph Jefferson Award, which honors excellence in Chicago-area theater.

**2008**   Boseman moves to Los Angeles and picks up more TV roles and a movie role in *The Express*.

**2011**   He lands the role of Jackie Robinson for the movie *42*. He also appears in the TV shows *Justified*, *Castle*, and *Fringe*.

**2016**   Boseman plays Black Panther for the first time in *Captain America: Civil War*.

**2017**   He works to raise money for Hurricane Harvey victims in Houston, Texas. Boseman speaks at the NAACP's annual conference, where he receives a nomination for the organization's Image Award. He praises pro football players who knelt, sat or raised a fist during the National Anthem in protest of President Donald Trump's comments that players who did so should be fired. Boseman tours the country promoting his new movie, *Marshall*.

## FILMOGRAPHY

**2018**   *Avengers: Infinity War*, T'Challa/Black Panther

**2018**   *Black Panther*, T'Challa/Black Panther

**2017**   *Marshall*, Thurgood Marshall

**2016**   *Message from the King*, Jacob King

**2016**   *Captain America: Civil War*, T'Challa/Black Panther

**2014**   *Get On Up*, James Brown

**2013**   *42*, Jackie Robinson

**Chapter One**
1. Phillips, Jevon. "Chadwick Boseman Explains How He Came up with Black Panther's Accent from the Fictional Land of Wakanda." *Los Angeles Times*, September 28, 2016.
2. Riesman, Abraham. "Ryan Coogler Physically Fought Chadwick Boseman on the Black Panther Set to Amp Him Up." *Vulture.com*, July 23, 2017.

**Chapter Two**
1. McDonald, Soraya Nadia. "Everything You Need To Know about Chadwick Boseman—Marvel's New Superhero, Black Panther." *Washington Post*, October 29, 2014.
2. T. L. Hanna 1995 High School Yearbook, Anderson, South Carolina.
3. Riley, Daniel. "The Surprisingly Sudden Arrival of Chadwick Boseman." *GQ*, September 22, 2014.
4. Ibid.
5. Ibid.

**Chapter 3**
1. Gregory, Sean. "Going Places with Chadwick Boseman." *Time*, February 21, 2013.
2. "Chadwick Boseman—The Distinguished Rise of Cinema's Next Champion." *Flaunt.com*, April 7, 2014.
3. Labrecque, Jeff. "Breaking Big: Welcome to The Show, Chadwick Boseman." *Entertainment Weekly*, November 20, 2014.
4. Gregory.
5. Ibid.
6. Ibid.
7. Miller, Julie. "*42* Star Chadwick Boseman on Playing Jackie Robinson, Copying His Baseball Moves, and Being Stood Up by the President." *Vanity Fair*, April 12, 2013.
8. Ibid.
9. Gregory.
10. "Chadwick Boseman—The Distinguished Rise of Cinema's Next Champion."

**Chapter 4**
1. Agard, Chancellor. "Marshall: Why Chadwick Boseman Decided to Play Another Historical Figure." *Entertainment Weekly*, August 15, 2017.
2. Hosley, Steve. "Star on the Rise: Chadwick Boseman." *Michigan Chronicle*, August 6, 2014.
3. Palladino, D.J. "Chadwick Boseman Is Proud to Be James Brown." *Santa Barbara Independent*, January 28, 2015.
4. Labrecque, Jeff. "Breaking Big: Welcome to The Show, Chadwick Boseman." *Entertainment Weekly*, November 20, 2014.
5. Golding, Shenequa. "Chadwick Boseman Brings Thurgood Marshall to Life in New Trailer 'Marshal.'" *Vibe*, June 22, 2017.
6. Hosley.
7. Palladino.

**Chapter Five**
1. Chadwick Boseman on Twitter. August 31, 2017. https://twitter.com/chadwickboseman/status/903279615564709888

2. Chadwick Boseman on Twitter. April 30, 2017. https://twitter.com/chadwickboseman/status/903027640977772544
3. Palladino, D.J. "Chadwick Boseman Is Proud to Be James Brown." *Santa Barbara Independent*, January 28, 2015.
4. Labrecque, Jeff. "Breaking Big: Welcome to The Show, Chadwick Boseman." *Entertainment Weekly*, November 20, 2014.
5. Riley, Daniel. "The Surprisingly Sudden Arrival of Chadwick Boseman." *GQ* Magazine, September 22, 2014.
6. Ibid.
7. Labrecque.
8. Riley.
9. Ibid.
10. Chadwick Boseman on Twitter. September 27, 2017. https://twitter.com/chadwickboseman/status/905890386626969600

## FURTHER READING

**Books**

Buckhanon, Kalisha (author). *Upstate: A Novel*. Chadwick Boseman and Heather Simms (Narrators). New York: Audio Book Renaissance, Holtzbrinck Publishers LLC. February 1, 2005.

Grimm, R.B. *Chadwick Boseman, Unauthorized & Uncensored*. Digital Edition V 1.0. Famous People Collection. Kindle edition. January 1, 2015.

Grimm, R.B. *Hollywood Actors Biographies Vol. 10: (Chadwick Boseman, Chandle Riggs, Channing Tatum, Charles Dance, Charles Halford, Charlie McDermott, Charlie Sheen, Charlie Weber, Chelan Simmons, Chelsea Handler)*. Kindle Edition. Digital Edition V 1.0. Actors Collection. July 6, 2015.

**Works Consulted**

Agard, Chancellor. "Marshall: Why Chadwick Boseman Decided to Play Another Historical Figure." *Entertainment Weekly*, August 15, 2017. http://ew.com/movies/2017/08/15/marshall-chadwick-boseman-interview/

Bui, Hoai-Tran. "Marshall Trailer: Chadwick Boseman Brings Justice as Thurgood Marshall in Biopic." *Slash Film*, September 1, 2017. http://www.slashfilm.com/marshall-trailer-chadwick-boseman-thurgood-marshall/

"Chadwick Boseman—The Distinguished Rise of Cinema's Next Champion." *Flaunt.com*, April 7, 2014. http://www.flaunt.com/content/people/chadwick-boseman

Foundas, Scott. "Film Review: *Get On Up*." *Variety*, July 28, 2014. http://variety.com/2014/film/reviews/film-review-get-on-up-1201268079/

Golding, Shenequa. "Chadwick Boseman Brings Thurgood Marshall to Life in New Trailer 'Marshall.'" *Vibe*, June 22, 2017. https://www.vibe.com/2017/06/chadwick-boseman-marshall-trailer/

Gregory, Sean. "Going Places with Chadwick Boseman." *Time*, February 21, 2013. http://style.time.com/2013/02/21/going-places-with-chadwick-boseman/

Hosley, Steve. "Star on the Rise: Chadwick Boseman." *Michigan Chronicle*, August 6, 2014. https://michronicleonline.com/2014/08/06/star-on-the-rise-chadwick-boseman/

Labrecque, Jeff. "Breaking Big: Welcome to The Show, Chadwick Boseman." *Entertainment Weekly*, November 20, 2014. http://ew.com/article/2014/11/20/chadwick-boseman-black-panther/

McDonald, Soraya Nadia. "Everything You Need to Know about Chadwick Boseman—Marvel's New Superhero, Black Panther." *Washington Post*, October 29, 2014. https://www.washingtonpost.com/news/morning-mix/wp/2014/10/29/everything-you-need-to-know-about-chadwick-boseman-marvels-new-superhero-black-panther/?utm_term=.d2fc4f2fe53f

Miller, Julie. "*42* Star Chadwick Boseman on Playing Jackie Robinson, Copying His Baseball Moves, and Being Stood Up by the President." *Vanity Fair*, April 12, 2013. https://www.vanityfair.com/hollywood/2013/04/chadwick-boseman-42-interview

Palladino, D.J. "Chadwick Boseman Is Proud to Be James Brown." *Santa Barbara Independent*, January 28, 2015. http://www.independent.com/news/2015/jan/28/chadwick-boseman-proud-be-james-brown/

Phillips, Jevon. "Chadwick Boseman Explains How He Came Up with Black Panther's Accent from the Fictional Land of Wakanda." *Los Angeles Times*, September 28, 2016. http://www.latimes.com/entertainment/herocomplex/la-et-hc-chadwick-boseman-black-panther-20160921-snap-story.html

Riesman, Abraham. "Ryan Coogler Physically Fought Chadwick Boseman on the Black Panther Set to Amp Him Up." *Vulture.com*, July 23, 2017. http://www.vulture.com/2017/07/ryan-coogler-fight-chadwick-boseman-black-panther-set.html

Riley, Daniel. "The Surprisingly Sudden Arrival of Chadwick Boseman." *GQ*, September 22, 2014. https://www.gq.com/story/chadwick-boseman

Tinubu, Aramida. "Before Black Panther, Chadwick Boseman Will Star in *Marshall*." *Ebony*, January 25, 2017. http://www.ebony.com/entertainment-culture/black-panther-chadwick-boseman-will-become-marshall#ixzz4rtpk627W

T. L. Hanna High School Parent Newsletter #47. "Hanna Grad Chad Boseman Plays Jackie Robinson in *42*." April 11, 2013. https://web.archive.org/web/20160304071919/http://www.anderson5.net/cms/lib02/SC01001931/Centricity/Domain/2867/Parent%20Newsletter%20April%2011%202013.pdf

Twitter: Chadwick Boseman. https://twitter.com/chadwickboseman

Yamato, Jen. "Chadwick Boseman Signed for 5 Films as Black Panther, Captain Marvel Bring Diversity to Superhero Slate." *Deadline Hollywood*, October 28, 2014. http://deadline.com/2014/10/marvel-black-panther-chadwick-boseman-black-female-superhero-movies-864294/

Yaniz, Robert, Jr. "Before 'Black Panther': 5 Best Chadwick Boseman Films (So Far)." *Cheatsheet.com*, July 31, 2017. https://www.cheatsheet.com/entertainment/black-panther-5-chadwick-boseman-films.html/?a=viewall

**On the Internet**

Best Marvel Comics for young readers
http://comicsalliance.com/marvel-comics-young-readers/

Black Panther movie trailer
https://www.youtube.com/watch?v=G5pHFvMQZCI

Marvel Comics games
http://www.marvelhq.com/

Marvel superheroes
http://marvel.com/characters

Top 100 Marvel characters
https://comicvine.gamespot.com/profile/theoptimist/lists/top-100-marvel-characters/32199/

**Academy Award** (ah-KAD-uh-mee ah-WARD)—An award given each year for several types of movie achievements, such as Best Actor, Best Original Screenplay, and Best Motion Picture.

**audition** (aw-DIH-shun)—A test given to actors to see if they are right for a movie or theater part.

**bigotry** (BIG-uh-tree)—Hatred or refusal to accept the members of a particular group.

**biopic** (BY-oh-pik)—A movie biography about a real person.

**choreographer** (kor-ee-AH-gruh-fer)—A person who comes up with dance moves and steps.

**civil rights movement** (SIH-vul RYTS MOOV-ment)—The nonviolent actions and plans that help bring about equal treatment for all people.

**debate** (dee-BAYT)—To discuss different points of view or opinions.

**depiction** (dee-PIK-shun)—The way something is shown.

**director** (der-EK-tur)—The person in charge of making a movie.

**fictional** (FIK-shuh-nul)—Made up or not true.

**general manager** (JEN-rul MAN-uh-jer)—The person in charge of the money and personnel decisions for a professional sports team.

**Little League Baseball**—A top youth baseball league in the United States.

**Major League Baseball**—The top professional baseball league in the United States.

**meteorite** (MEE-tee-or-yt)—A rock from outer space that passes through Earth's atmosphere and crashes onto the surface.

**National Forensic League** (NAH-shuh-nul for-EN-zik LEEG)—A national speech and debate organization that helps students learn and grow as public speakers.

**National Honor Society**—A nationwide organization that honors high school students who excel in grades, leadership, character, and service to others.

**nominate** (NAH-mih-nayt)—To name or select for a position or office.

**racial slur** (RAY-shul SLUR)—An insult to a group of people based on the color of their skin.

**retractable** (ree-TRAK-tih-bul)—Able to be drawn in as well as extended, like a claw.

**segregation** (seh-greh-GAY-shun)—The act of separating one group of people from another.

**superhero** (SOO-per-hee-roh)—A person who is able to help others because he or she has abilities beyond that of a normal person.

**upholstery** (uh-POHL-stree)—Materials such as cushions, coils, and springs used in furniture.

**vibranium** (vy-BRAY-nee-um)—A fictional metal created by Marvel Comics. It is far stronger than ordinary metals because it absorbs sound.